WORKBOOK

JACK HIBBS

CALLED TO TAKE A BOLD STAND

HARVEST HOUSE PUBLISHERS
EUGENE, OREGON

Cover design by Bryce Williamson and Kyler Dougherty

Cover images © JMGehrke, jeewan chandra, enjoynz / Getty Images

Interior design by KUHN Design Group

For bulk, special sales, or ministry purchases, please call 1-800-547-8979.
Email: CustomerService@hhpbooks.com

Called to Take a Bold Stand Workbook
Copyright © 2025 by Jack Hibbs
Published by Harvest House Publishers
Eugene, Oregon 97408
www.harvesthousepublishers.com

ISBN 978-0-7369-9156-8 (pbk)
ISBN 978-0-7369-9157-5 (eBook)

Printed in the United States of America

25 26 27 28 29 30 31 32 33 / BP / 10 9 8 7 6 5 4 3 2 1

CONTENTS

PART 1: YOU HAVE WHAT IT TAKES

1. The Real You 7
2. Believe 15
3. Bear His Image 23
4. Remember 31
5. Be Confident 37

PART 2: WATCH OUT

6. Watch and Listen 47
7. In Your Sights 53
8. It's Dark Out There 59
9. Urgent, Urgent, Urgent! 67
10. The False and the True 73

PART 3: GOING PUBLIC

11. What Are You Waiting For? 81
12. Today Is the Best Day 89
13. Heading for Home 95
14. Before I Let You Go 103

PART 1

YOU HAVE WHAT IT TAKES

LESSON 1

THE REAL YOU

> Our biblical beliefs are under full-scale attack, and it is time to take a biblical stand because history teaches that there can be no neutrality when it comes to war. Hostile aggression demands decisive action. For us to be victorious, we must know ourselves and the One who has enlisted us into this bold faith.
>
> *Called to Take a Bold Stand*, page 14

Taking a bold stand requires that we be informed. This means having a clear understanding of who we are in Christ. When we realize how our Lord has transformed and equipped us, we will come to know the resources God has given us for waging spiritual battle. And the better we understand what the Lord desires of us, the more effectively we will be able to respond with wisdom and conviction to attacks upon our beliefs.

Yes, this means preparation. It means doing what is necessary so we are ready to face whatever challenges come our way. The apostle Paul was forthright about this. In 2 Timothy 2:3, he wrote, "You therefore must endure hardship as a good soldier of Jesus Christ."

The word "hardship" speaks of pain, suffering, and spiritual warfare. These are inevitable because we live in a hostile, evil world. However, Scripture repeatedly reminds us that God rewards those who are faithful to Him. In 2 Thessalonians 3:3, we read that "the Lord is faithful. He will establish you and guard you against the evil one." What an incredible promise! God says He will care for us and protect us.

Though we can expect hardship, we have no reason to be fearful. God has equipped us and will sustain us. He hasn't left us in the dark about how we can take a bold stand. He has lovingly given us an abundance of instructions and encouragement, all of which we should take to heart.

GROWING BOLDER

As you answer the following questions, you'll want to have your Bible in hand, as well as your copy of the book *Called to Take a Bold Stand.*

1. What are the three great spiritual enemies of every Christian? (See page 13.)

2. What are the two primary goals of these three enemies? (See page 13.)

3. Why do you think identifying the enemy is such an important aspect of being effective in spiritual battle?

4. On page 14 of *Called to Take a Bold Stand*, we read that "hostile aggression demands decisive action." Why do you think this is the case?

YOU ARE CALLED TO STAND

5. What does it mean to take a bold stand? (See page 15.)

6. What happens when we do anything less than taking a bold stand? (See page 15.)

7. What is the challenge for every Christ-follower today? (See page 15.)

8. Why should we say yes to this challenge? (See page 16.)

9. On page 16 of *Called to Take a Bold Stand*, we read that "what you do now matters in eternity." What types of things do you think count for eternity? What types of things do you think are worthless from an eternal perspective?

YOU ARE IN CHRIST

10. On page 16 of *Called to Take a Bold Stand*, we read, "For better or worse, people will make assessments about us based on what they observe regarding our Christianity." Has your faith changed you? How would the people around you answer that question?

11. When it comes to letting your faith change you, where do you see room for growth?

YOU HAVE A NEW NATURE

12. What does the title *Christian* mean? (See page 17.)

13. Why is our faith precious, according to 2 Peter 1:1? (See page 18.)

14. On page 19 of *Called to Take a Bold Stand*, we read, "When your faith is in Jesus Christ, you are hidden in Him." What do you think it looks like for a Christian to be "hidden" in Christ?

15. Read Galatians 2:20. How does the apostle Paul describe what it means to be hidden in Christ?

16. Read 2 Corinthians 5:17. If you call yourself a Christian yet there has been little to no change in your life, why should you be concerned?

You've Been Transformed

17. What promise did Jesus give in Acts 1:4-5—a promise that applies to every believer?

18. What do the following passages say about you as a Christian?

a. 1 Corinthians 6:19—

b. Ephesians 4:30—

You've Been Set Free

19. How did Paul, Timothy, Epapharas, James, Peter, and Jude see themselves first and foremost? (See page 24.)

20. The English word translated "bondservant" comes from the Greek word *doulos*, or "slave." As those who are bondservants of Christ, what attitude should we have toward our master? (See page 26.)

21. From an earthly perspective, the term *slave* is negative. But from a biblical perspective, why do you think it is a positive thing to view ourselves as bondservants or slaves of Christ?

22. As a bondservant, Christ is a model of what it means to live sacrificially. What can we learn from His example?

YOUR TIME IS NOW

23. Psalm 90:12 says, "Teach us to number our days, that we might gain a heart of wisdom." What are some specific ways you can ask God to help you to number your days wisely?

PUTTING YOUR BOLD STAND INTO ACTION

24. On page 23 of *Called to Take a Bold Stand*, we read,

> By God's grace, with the Holy Spirit's help, you are different from where you started in Christ, and you're bringing things like pride, lust, or anger under the control of the Spirit. You are growing in the grace and knowledge of Jesus Christ and advancing in your faith. Second Corinthians 3:18 announces that you are "being transformed…from glory to glory," but this transformation isn't a one-and-done event. It is an ongoing and observable work of the Holy Spirit.

God's work of transforming your life is an ongoing process. In what ways has He been bringing about change in you recently?

25. Philippians 2:5-7 says, "Let this mind be in you which was also in Christ Jesus, who, being in the form of God, did not consider it robbery to be equal with God, but made Himself of no reputation, taking the form of a bondservant, and coming in the likeness of men."

a. When Christ came to Earth, He took on "the form of a bondservant"—He came to serve. What did He give up when He left heaven?

b. In light of the sacrifices Christ made on our behalf, how can we best respond?

LESSON 2

BELIEVE

> A true sense of purpose influences how we live because, without real direction or meaning, we tend to drift aimlessly, never finding true satisfaction. Sadly, many people live like that, and frustration and despair are the unfortunate results. I don't believe that a born-again believer can or should live without knowledge of God's plans for them. While it is impossible to anticipate all that God has in store for you, knowing that He has a plan should fill you with excitement, awe, and energizing faith!
>
> *Called to Take a Bold Stand*, page 29

When we take the time to study the Bible and learn God's plans for us, we will gain a true sense of purpose. It's when we line ourselves up with God's desires that we are able to point our lives in the right direction, make the best use of our time and abilities, and experience incredible satisfaction.

God has a purpose for every one of us. There is nothing accidental about where He has placed us in life. He has given every one of us a sphere of influence. And it's not the size of our sphere that matters, but whether we make good use of the opportunities God has given us.

In the times when you feel inadequate or insignificant, you can find encouragement in the truths that in Christ, you are complete, you are family, God's nature is in you, and you have no reason to be ashamed.

Every one of these truths is backed by promises—promises that God is at work in you, and according to Philippians 1:6, "He who has begun a good work in you will complete it." There is never a moment when God is inactive in our lives. He is building us, shaping us, strengthening us so that we can fulfill the calling He has given to us.

Comparing ourselves to others is a sure recipe for dissatisfaction. Instead, we need to focus on what and who we are in Christ. And we need to remember that a true sense of direction and purpose comes solely from yielding ourselves to God wholeheartedly.

GROWING BOLDER

As you answer the following questions, you'll want to have your Bible in hand, as well as your copy of the book *Called to Take a Bold Stand.*

GOD'S PURPOSES COME WITH PROMISES

God told Jeremiah, "Before I formed you in the womb I knew you; before you were born I sanctified you; I ordained you a prophet to the nations" (Jeremiah 1:5). And in Psalm 139:16, King David wrote,

> Your eyes saw my substance, being yet unformed.
> And in Your book they all were written,
> the days fashioned for me,
> when as yet there were none of them.

1. According to those two passages, to what extent is God involved in our lives even before we are born?

2. Knowing this, how much do you think God is involved in your life now?

3. The God of the universe cares for you greatly. How should this truth affect your perspective on the circumstances you face each day in life?

4. According to Psalm 139:16, "all" our days were written in God's book before we were born. What does this say about how intentional God is when He works in our lives?

5. Second Corinthians 3:5 says, "Our sufficiency is from God." In all that we do, why should our confidence be in God and not in ourselves?

6. Read 2 Corinthians 12:9. Why should we not let our weaknesses cause us to think we are useless to God?

GOD PROMISES:

You Are Complete

7. What assurance are we given in Colossians 2:10?

8. How much divine power does 2 Peter 1:2-3 say we are given access to? (See page 33.)

9. Read 2 Timothy 3:17. What does this passage promise God's Word can do for us?

10. We are complete in Christ, the Lord's divine power has given to us all things that pertain to life and godliness, and the Bible can equip us for every good work. In what ways do these truths encourage you?

You Are Family

11. According to Romans 8:15-16, God has adopted us, chosen us, made us His children. What does the fact God is our Father and we are His children communicate about the nature of the relationship we have with Him?

12. Ephesians 1:5 (NLT) says, "God decided in advance to adopt us into His own family by bringing us to Himself through Jesus Christ. This is what He wanted to do, and it gave Him great pleasure."

    a. In what ways do we see the extent of God's love for us communicated in this passage?

    b. What does this say about how God views you?

13. Children of human parents have certain privileges available to them. What are some of the privileges we have available to us as God's children?

His Nature Is in You

14. When 2 Peter 1:4 says we "share [God's] divine nature," it's not saying we're little gods, but that we are enabled to manifest His characteristics. What are those characteristics, according to…

    a. Galatians 5:22-23?

    b. Philippians 2:1-4?

    c. 1 Corinthians 13:4-7?

You Will Not Be Ashamed

15. Second Peter 1:5 exhorts us to "add to your faith virtue." How does the Western world typically define virtue? From a biblical standpoint, what is virtue? (See page 40.)

16. On page 41 of *Called to Take a Bold Stand*, we read, "You need to stand for what you know is absolute truth." What is the best way for us to know when to take a stand on an issue, and why?

17. The world is quick to shame those who disagree with it. But who should we seek to please, and why, according to…

    a. 2 Corinthians 5:9-10?

    b. Galatians 1:10?

    c. Timothy 2:3-4?

PUTTING YOUR BOLD STAND INTO ACTION

18. Second Peter 1:4 says God has given us "exceedingly great and precious promises." Share two or three promises you've experienced personally, and how they've been fulfilled in your life.

19. As Colossians 2:10 says, we are complete in Christ. To get a better sense of what this means, answer this question: What can Christ give you that the world cannot?

20. Because Christ is in us, our thoughts, words, and actions ought to shine His characteristics to the people around us. According to the following passages, what is required of us to make this possible?

    a. John 15:4-5—

    b. Galatians 5:22-23—

    c. Colossians 3:16—

LESSON 3

BEAR HIS IMAGE

California is home to the oldest, tallest, and largest trees on the planet...While General Sherman is not the oldest or tallest, it is the largest tree by volume...nothing is bigger than this behemoth. Standing 275 feet tall with a 36-foot circumference, it consumes 1,000 gallons of water every 24 hours. General Sherman's bark grows at a rate that equals a 60-foot ponderosa pine every year. Some say you can almost hear the massive giant growing.

It is hard to believe, but General Sherman's life began with a tiny seed the size of a pinhead. When that seed fell into the ground and died, it initiated the growth we see today. Stored within Sherman's seed was the DNA data it needed to advance toward maturity until it became the fulfillment of what God designed it to be. I cannot think of a better picture of the sanctification process of growth in the believer's life.

Called to Take a Bold Stand, pages 43-44

As we mature spiritually, God's design is for us to grow more like Christ. In Romans 8:29, we are told, "Whom God foreknew, He also predestined to be conformed to the image of His Son." In 1 Corinthians 11:1, Paul urges his readers, "Imitate me, just as I also imitate Christ."

When we are saved, we are justified in Christ. God declares us to be righteous through our faith in Christ, who took our sin upon Him and placed His righteousness upon us. We are not saved by anything we do, but rather, by what Christ has done for us.

After we are justified, we grow in sanctification. This means we mature and become more like Jesus, bearing the image of the One whom we call our Lord.

Sanctification doesn't happen instantly. Growth occurs as we read the Bible and apply its truths and principles to our lives. The apostle Paul calls us to "cleanse ourselves from all filthiness of the flesh and spirit, perfecting holiness in the fear of God" (2 Corinthians 7:1). This happens as we allow Christ to "sanctify and cleanse [us] with the washing of water by the word" (Ephesians 5:26).

The best part of becoming more like Christ is stated in Philippians 1:6: "He who has begun a good work in you will complete it until the day of Jesus Christ." Day by day, God is perfecting us. We need only to yield to His transforming work in our lives.

GROWING BOLDER

As you answer the following questions, you'll want to have your Bible in hand, as well as your copy of the book *Called to Take a Bold Stand.*

BEARING HIS IMAGE BY GROWING

1. On page 44 of *Called to Take a Bold Stand*, we read that sanctification is "growth in Christ that brings about a spiritually complete person." In what areas of your life do you see growth taking place right now?

2. What negative side effects do you think we are likely to experience when we're not pursuing spiritual growth?

3. What is God's will for us, according to 1 Thessalonians 4:3?

4. On page 46 of *Called to Take a Bold Stand*, we read, "Through sanctification, God gradually removes from us the controlling passions of this world and replaces them with a Christ-centered way of living." What are two or three examples of this you've seen in your own life?

5. What are some examples of challenges we face as we seek to grow spiritually mature?

BEARING HIS IMAGE BY BEING FRUITFUL

6. To become more like Christ requires that we yield to what He wants to do in our lives. What are some examples of ways we tend to resist the work He is doing in us?

7. Read John 15:5 and answer the following:

   a. What do you think it means to abide in Christ? (For help with this answer, see 1 John 2:5 and 1 John 3:24.)

   b. What does John 15:5 say is the result of abiding in Christ?

c. What is the inevitable result of not abiding in Christ?

8. When it comes to bearing fruit in the Christian life, 2 Peter 1:5 says we are to be "giving all diligence." What does that tell us?

Self-Controlled Perseverance

9. Second Peter 1:5-6 calls us to be diligent about pursuing self-control. Why do you think self-control is such an important characteristic in the Christian life?

Godliness and Brotherly Kindness

10. Godliness is a righteousness that mimics God or Christ. Why do you think it's true that the more you imitate Christ, the more God is able to use you?

11. To show brotherly kindness to others is to express godly affection for them. What are some ways we can show brotherly kindness to others?

12. According to Matthew 5:44 and Romans 12:21, how far should we be willing to go when it comes to exhibiting kindness?

Greater Love

13. What is agape love? (See pages 51-52.)

14. What are some practical ways we can show agape love, according to 1 Corinthians 13:4-7?

15. What does 1 John 4:9-11 tell us about God's love? What can we learn from God's example?

16. Why is the oneness and love that Christians show to one another so important, according to John 17:21-23?

BEARING HIS IMAGE BY INVESTING

17. Read 2 Peter 1:8. In relation to our spiritual growth, what does being "barren" and "unfruitful" indicate about us?

18. On page 54 of *Called to Take a Bold Stand*, we read, "To be unfruitful is to be unproductive and not invested. When it comes to faith, the more you invest, the better the results will be." What are two or three examples of how God has been teaching you this principle?

19. Why is it dangerous for us to compare ourselves to others when it comes to how we invest in the kingdom? (See page 57.)

PUTTING YOUR BOLD STAND INTO ACTION

20. Romans 12:1-2 says, "I beseech you therefore, brethren, by the mercies of God, that you present your bodies a living sacrifice, holy, acceptable to God, which is your reasonable service. And do not be conformed to this world, but be transformed by the renewing of your mind, that you may prove what is that good and acceptable and perfect will of God."

    a. What are we to present our bodies as?

    b. What are we to avoid conforming to?

    c. How does transformation take place?

    d. How do you think mind renewal takes place? (For hints, see John 17:17 and Ephesians 5:26.)

    e. What is the result of being a living sacrifice and having a renewed mind?

21. According to the following passages, what kind of fruit should we desire to grow in our lives?

    The fruit of our words

    Proverbs 15:1-2—

    Proverbs 16:24—

    Ephesians 4:29—

    Ephesians 5:4—

    The fruit of our attitudes

    Galatians 5:22-23—

    Philippians 2:14-15—

    Philippians 4:8—

    Colossians 3:12—

The fruit of our actions

Matthew 5:16—

Colossians 1:10—

Colossians 3:23—

Titus 3:8, 14—

LESSON 4

REMEMBER

> I have heard it said that the best defense against false teaching is true living. I say, "Amen" to that! A church filled with growing Christians, strong in faith, will not likely fall prey to counterfeit Christianity. But that presupposes that the Christians build their lives on the authoritative Word of God. Christians who rely on experience, at the expense of truth, find themselves in dangerous territory. False teachers cunningly target people who shun solid Bible learning in favor of experiences. And when you add the temptation of worldly alternatives, it's no wonder that Jude and other New Testament writers felt compelled to remind us of the essentials concerning our faith again and again and again. We need the reinforcement of biblical truth!
>
> *Called to Take a Bold Stand*, page 61

There's a reason God states specific truths in the Bible repeatedly: He wants us to remember them.

In Ephesians 4, the apostle Paul wrote about the importance of leaders within the church "equipping...the saints for the work of ministry, for the edifying of the body of Christ" so that we can grow in unity and knowledge, "to the measure of the stature of the fullness of Christ" (verses 12-13). Why this emphasis on equipping and edifying? So "that we should no longer be children, tossed to and fro and carried about with every wind of doctrine, by the trickery of men, in the cunning craftiness of deceitful plotting" (verse 14).

The more we anchor ourselves in God's Word—which equips and edifies us—the less likely we are to stumble or go adrift. That's why it's essential for us to go to churches where the Bible is taught clearly and accurately. And that's why it's vital that we make a habit of feeding upon God's Word and taking it to heart. When we are deliberate about grounding ourselves in biblical truth, we will stand strong. We won't become vulnerable to the latest false doctrines and human wisdom that happens to be infiltrating the church.

And it's not enough to merely learn biblical truths. We need to dwell on those truths repeatedly so that we are constantly mindful of them and don't forget them.

That is how we can best protect ourselves in a world filled with deception.

GROWING BOLDER

As you answer the following questions, you'll want to have your Bible in hand, as well as your copy of the book *Called to Take a Bold Stand.*

FIGHT FOR YOUR FAITH

1. When Jude said to "contend earnestly for the faith," who was he writing to? (See page 60.)

2. According to Matthew 24:11, what is one of the primary reasons we need to be prepared to contend for the faith? (See page 60.)

YOUR FAITH IS IN CHRIST

3. Read 2 Peter 1:12-15. In this passage, how many times did Peter use variations of the word *remind*? What does this tell us about the importance of remembering key truths?

4. What was Peter especially eager to ensure, according to verse 15?

5. In light of what Isaiah 40:8 says, what is the greatest legacy we can give to those who look to us for guidance?

6. What do we learn about God's Word from Hebrews 4:12? (See page 65.)

YOUR FAITH ISN'T IN A SYSTEM

7. What is our sole means for accessing God, according to John 14:6?

8. If anyone could have pleased God through their religious achievements, it would have been the apostle Paul. Read Philippians 3:4-6. From a human perspective, what made Paul so special? Once Paul became a Christian, how did he view his accomplishments? (See verses 7-8.)

9. How do the following passages affirm that our faith isn't in a system?

   a. Romans 1:16—

   b. Ephesians 2:8-9—

c. Titus 3:5—

YOUR FAITH IS PRACTICAL

10. As explained in *Called to Take a Bold Stand*, what does it mean to "drill down on the truth"? (See page 68.)

11. On page 69 in *Called to Take a Bold Stand*, we read that "our conduct is where our beliefs are shown to be genuine or not." Why do you think that is true?

12. Read Titus 2:11-12. What does the grace of God teach us to do?

13. In light of what you've learned so far, what are two or three reasons it's so important for our faith to be visible to those around us?

RENEW FAITH'S PERSPECTIVE

14. Noah, Abraham, and Sarah are mentioned in the hall of faith in Hebrews 11. What did they do that made them noteworthy? (See page 70.)

15. Noah, Abraham, and Sarah were willing to put faith to the test. What advice do the following passages give us for those times when our own faith is tested?

    a. Joshua 1:9—

    b. Proverbs 3:5-6—

    c. Philippians 4:6-7—

    d. James 1:2-4—

PUTTING YOUR BOLD STAND INTO ACTION

16. There are some who say that when you follow Christ, life will become easier. But that's not what the Bible teaches. All through the ages, Christians have faced difficulties and persecution for their faith. Jesus Himself was clear about the cost of following Him: "If anyone desires to come after Me, let him deny himself, and take up his cross daily, and follow Me." He also warned, "In the world you will have tribulation" (John 16:33).

    a. In what ways have you experienced the cost of following Christ?

    b. Where do you see room for growth when it comes to enduring this cost?

c. Why is it worthwhile for us to endure this cost, according to the following passages?

Romans 8:17—

Romans 8:18—

Romans 8:31-39—

17. On page 72 of *Called to Take a Bold Stand*, we read, "We all need passion—hot hearts—for God, that translates into determination, meaning, and purpose. Imagine if we found Jesus, stood for Jesus, and caught fire for Jesus. Only then would we be undeterred and unstoppable!"

We are then encouraged to "get up every morning and say, 'Lord Jesus, I don't know how many days I have left, but I want to use them well. I'm all in with whatever You have for me today.'"

a. In your current circumstances, what would it look like for you to be "all in"?

b. If you knew you didn't have many days left, what would be your top priorities?

c. How could you put one of these priorities into practice right now?

LESSON 5

BE CONFIDENT

> It is important to understand that the Bible's unchanging truth, as it is lived out individually, is also subjective because *how* it affects us is personal. You and I can agree that "He who has begun a good work in you will complete it" (Philippians 1:6) is a fact, knowing that how God chooses to complete the work in us will differ. Unlike questionable sources, God's objective and subjective truths—perfectly coupled—allow us to draw sound conclusions with confidence.
>
> *Called to Take a Bold Stand*, page 77

As Christians, we can live with great confidence because God, who possesses infinite power and wisdom, backs every promise and proclamation given in His Word. Our salvation is secure, for nothing can snatch us out of Jesus' hands (John 10:28-29). There is nothing that can separate us from God's love (Romans 8:35-39). God has said He will never leave nor forsake us (Hebrews 13:5). We have already been given the gift of eternal life (Romans 6:23), and we can know with certainty that someday, we will be glorified (Romans 8:30). The Holy Spirit dwells in us (1 Corinthians 3:16), guides us in truth (John 16:13), and helps us in our weakness, interceding for us in prayer (Romans 8:26).

All this and much more is ours because we belong to God and He is at work in us. God never fails to keep His promises, and He is unchanging. He is completely trustworthy. Can you see why, of all people, Christians can be the most confident of all?

This confidence should have an impact on how we live.

GROWING BOLDER

As you answer the following questions, you'll want to have your Bible in hand, as well as your copy of the book *Called to Take a Bold Stand*.

CONFIDENT IN THE FACTS

1. In what ways do the following facts in Scripture give you confidence?

   a. Nothing can snatch us from Jesus' hands (John 10:28-29)—

   b. Nothing can separate us from God's love (Romans 8:35-39)—

   c. God will never leave nor forsake us (Hebrews 13:5)—

   d. The gift of eternal life is already ours (Romans 6:23)—

   e. The Holy Spirit dwells in us and will guide us in all truth (1 Corinthians 6:19; John 16:13)—

f. The Holy Spirit prays for us and helps us in our weaknesses (Romans 8:26)—

2. List three or four other facts in the Bible that are especially dear to you:

3. What do the following passages tell you about God's trustworthiness?

   a. 1 Kings 8:56—

   b. 2 Corinthians 1:20—

   c. James 1:17—

4. Philippians 1:6 says, "He who has begun a good work in you will complete it." In what ways does this promise build your confidence?

THE CONFIDENCE OF EYEWITNESSES

5. In Acts 1:3, Luke said that eyewitnesses saw "many infallible proofs" that backed what Jesus taught and did. What level of confidence is communicated by Luke's use of the word "infallible"?

6. Read 1 John 1:1-2. Why were the apostles able to be so bold about what they proclaimed?

7. According to 2 Peter 1:16, what can we be certain of regarding Jesus Christ?

8. What does Isaiah 55:10-11 say about the reliability of God's Word?

Seeing Transformation

9. Read Matthew 17:2. On the Mount of Transfiguration, what did Peter, James, and John see happen to Jesus?

10. According to Matthew 17:5, what did the three men hear God proclaim?

11. How do you think this experience affected the way Peter, James, and John perceived Jesus?

Seeing Power

12. While Jesus was on Earth, He humbled Himself and was willing to die on a cross. Some people equate meekness with weakness. But what is the biblical definition of *meekness*? (See page 81.)

13. The Roman soldiers mocked Jesus as He hung on the cross because they thought He was powerless. But according to the following passages, in what ways was Christ's power made evident at the cross?

    a. 1 Corinthians 1:18—

    b. Colossians 2:15—

    c. Hebrews 2:14—

14. According to Matthew 28:18, what end result was made possible because Christ went to the cross?

15. Read Revelation 1:17-18. What does this passage tell us about the extent of Christ's power?

16. In response to Christ's power and what He accomplished at the cross, what do the angels and living creatures in heaven say Christ is worthy of? (See Revelation 5:12-13.)

17. Why were the disciples willing to die for Christ? (See page 83.)

THE CONFIDENCE OF INFALLIBLE PROOF

18. According to 2 Peter 1:19, we have "a more sure word of prophecy." In light of this, how should we respond, according to the rest of verse 19? (See page 84.)

19. The apostles were eyewitnesses of the resurrected Christ. How many other witnesses verified the fact Christ rose from the dead? (See 1 Corinthians 15:6 and page 86.)

20. Why is this evidence for Christ's resurrection so important, according to 1 Corinthians 15:14-19?

PUT IT TO THE TEST

Test upon Test: The Honesty Test

21. What is the honesty test, and in what ways do we witness the honesty of the Bible? (See pages 87-88.)

Test upon Test: The Telephone Test

22. According to what we read on page 88 of *Called to Take a Bold Stand*, how big is the gap between the original manuscripts and existing copies of…

    Pliny the Younger's works?

    Caesar's account of the Gallic Wars?

Plato's *Tetrologies*?

23. By comparison, what is the time gap between the original manuscripts and existing copies of the New Testament? (See page 88.)

Test upon Test: The Number of Copies Extant Test

24. How many extant supporting copies are there of the New Testament, and which manuscript is next in line? (See page 89.) What does this tell you about the evidence for the reliability of Scripture?

Test upon Test: The Corroboration Test

25. What kind of ancient evidence is available apart from the Bible that confirms the life, actions, and death and resurrection of Jesus? (See pages 89-90.)

MOVE FORWARD WITH CONFIDENCE

26. One evidence for the reliability of the Bible that many skeptics overlook is the effect it has on the lives of those who believe it.

    a. How has the Bible changed your life?

b. If you wanted to convince a loved one or friend of the Bible's power to change lives, what would you say?

PUTTING YOUR BOLD STAND INTO ACTION

27. What do the following passages say about the reliability of God's Word?

    a. Psalm 119:89—

    b. Isaiah 55:10-11—

    c. Matthew 24:35—

    d. 2 Timothy 3:16—

28. Which two or three promises in God's Word mean the most to you, and how have they built your confidence as a Christian?

PART 2

WATCH OUT

LESSON 6

WATCH AND LISTEN

Well-trained soldiers not only understand their environment and its dynamics, they also intend to win. Ancient Chinese warrior Sun Tzu put it like this: "Victorious warriors win first and then go to war, while defeated warriors go to war first and then seek to win." Did you know Jesus made that same point? He said nobody goes into battle until they first figure out that they've got the wherewithal to not only engage in a war, but also to finish it. "What king, going to make war against another king, does not sit down first and consider whether he is able with ten thousand to meet him who comes against him with twenty thousand?" (Luke 14:31). Christian, behind you are all the resources of heaven. You have what it takes!

Called to Take a Bold Stand, page 96

Satan is eager to do everything he can to weaken the church. That is why he infiltrates it with false teachers and worldly philosophies that undermine biblical teaching. And it's why he does all he can to seduce Christians to be complacent or to indulge in sin. Satan knows that a weak church filled with Christians who are preoccupied by worldly pursuits is no threat to him.

This is why we need to be so vigilant and watchful. The church is to boldly proclaim the gospel and shine God's light into the darkness that envelops this world. We are to be pure and to hold fervently to the truth. And when we are diligent about doing what God has called us to do, we can expect Satan will attack. He doesn't like strong and healthy churches and Christians.

When we place ourselves on the front lines of what God is doing in our world, we will find ourselves in the crosshairs of the enemy. While it is never easy to engage in spiritual warfare, we can know with absolute certainty that God has our backs. We have no reason to be fearful because "He who is in you is greater than he who is in the world" (1 John 4:4).

GROWING BOLDER

As you answer the following questions, you'll want to have your Bible in hand, as well as your copy of the book *Called to Take a Bold Stand.*

1. Why does it make sense that the devil does not care about a sleepy, carnal, lethargic church? (See page 97.)

FALSE TEACHERS ABOUND

Watch Out for Wolves

2. What can we be certain of, according to the following passages?

   a. Matthew 24:4-5—

   b. Acts 20:28-29—

   c. 2 Peter 2:1—

3. Read the following passages. What is the Bible able to do in people's lives?

   a. Colossians 1:5-6—

   b. 2 Timothy 3:16-17—

4. With the above answers in mind, why do you think Satan is so eager to attack and undermine the Bible?

Watch Out for Counterfeits

5. What does 1 Thessalonians 5:21-22 urge us to do?

6. What exhortation are we given in 2 Timothy 2:15?

7. What important lesson does Jesus give us about teachers in Matthew 7:15-20?

Watch Out for Believable Lies

8. There are some teachers who say things that sound good but, in reality, are lies. They

promote believable lies. What are two or three examples of believable lies you've heard—lies that sound good on the surface but are actually unbiblical?

9. For those who might think spiritual error isn't all that harmful, what warning does Galatians 5:9 give?

10. What should doubt drive us to do? (See pages 101-102.)

11. A key reason for making sure we're attending a church that is faithful to God's Word is so we can be led by pastors and teachers who will equip and edify us (Ephesians 4:11-13). When we do this, what are we able to avoid, according to verse 14?

Watch Out for Killers of the Soul

12. One way false teachers do great harm is by giving messages that please crowds instead of proclaiming a clear gospel message that leads to salvation in Christ alone. What fact did Jesus state in John 14:6?

13. What is essential for becoming saved, according to Romans 10:9?

14. What warning did Paul give in Galatians 1:8-9?

15. Read Romans 1:16. What does the gospel alone have the power to do?

Watch Out for Exploiters

16. According to the following passages, what are some characteristics of false teachers?

    a. Romans 16:17-18—

    b. 2 Timothy 6:3-5—

    c. 2 Peter 2:1-3—

17. The false prophets in Jeremiah's day told people not to worry about God's judgment. What are some incorrect teachings that today's false teachers proclaim about sin and judgment?

JUDGMENT IS COMING!

18. How does Jude describe false teachers in verses 12 and 13?

19. At the end of verse 13, what does Jude say about the destiny of false prophets?

20. What do false teachers bring upon themselves, according to 2 Peter 2:1?

21. On page 108 of *Called to Take a Bold Stand*, we read, "You won't realize your need for a Savior until you recognize that you are a sinner." There are some who say it is unloving to tell people they are sinners. But why is doing this actually the most loving thing we can do?

PUTTING YOUR BOLD STAND INTO ACTION

22. What are some good ways to discern whether a church, pastor, teacher, or Christian author is or is not being faithful to God's Word?

23. Why does it make sense that a faithful Bible teacher would be diligent about moral purity, whereas a false teacher wouldn't?

24. Why is it important for us to encourage and show gratitude to those who are faithful to God's Word?

LESSON 7

IN YOUR SIGHTS

> Jesus said, "Enter by the narrow gate; for wide is the gate and broad is the way that leads to destruction, and there are many who go in by it. Because narrow is the gate and difficult is the way which leads to life, and there are few who find it. Beware of false prophets" (Matthew 7:13-15). Notice that false prophets are directly connected to the broad way to hell, which is why we need to set them in our sights and determine to catch, defeat, and overcome them.
>
> *Called to Take a Bold Stand*, page 112

Many Christians assume that the greatest danger faced by a church is ungodly influences from outside its walls. But there is far greater danger from within—from those who infiltrate a church, claim to represent Christ, and spread error disguised as truth. Second Timothy 3:4-5 describes such predators as "lovers of pleasure rather than lovers of God, having a form of godliness but denying its power." They appear godly but aren't. The rest of verse 5 admonishes us to turn away from such people.

All through the New Testament, there are many warnings about false teachers who will embed themselves within churches and deceive people. The fact Scripture speaks repeatedly about this indicates how serious the problem would be all through the church age. With the warnings are fierce condemnations that reveal how strongly God despises false teachers. They malign the truth, misrepresent Christ, and keep people on the broad path to spiritual destruction.

False teachers are deadly because they promote a counterfeit Christianity that keeps people out of heaven. The words Jesus spoke to the false religious leaders of His day apply to today's false teachers as well: "Woe to you, scribes and Pharisees, hypocrites! For you are like whitewashed tombs which indeed appear beautiful outwardly, but inside are full of dead men's bones and all uncleanness. Even so you also outwardly appear righteous to men, but inside you are full of hypocrisy and lawlessness" (Matthew 23:27-28).

GROWING BOLDER

As you answer the following questions, you'll want to have your Bible in hand, as well as your copy of the book *Called to Take a Bold Stand.*

WE CANNOT IGNORE THE FACTS

1. Why should we not ignore false teachers? (See pages 112-113.)

2. What is one of the reasons unbelievers criticize the church today? (See page 113.)

HOW BAD COULD THEY BE?

They Are Prideful

3. Why do you think we can legitimately say pride is perhaps the most dangerous sin of all?

4. Why is a false teacher's disdain for authority not surprising? (See pages 114-115.)

5. What exhortations are we given in the following passages?

   a. Philippians 2:3-4—

   b. Colossians 3:12-13—

   c. James 4:6—

They Are Presumptuous

6. What does it mean to be presumptuous? (See page 115.)

7. In contrast, how does 1 Corinthians 6:20 urge us to live, and why? (See page 116.)

8. Consider the fact false teachers despise God's authority and His Word. What kind of behavior can we expect from someone who has no fear of God?

They Are Depraved

9. What are false teachers guilty of, according to 2 Peter 2:10-12?

10. What does it mean to tell a false teacher that "God is in hot pursuit of you"? (See page 118.)

11. What do the following passages say about God and the wicked?

    a. Psalm 5:5—

    b. Psalm 7:11—

    c. Proverbs 6:16-18—

    d. Proverbs 15:9—

12. What does Hebrews 6:4-6 say to false teachers? (See page 119.)

13. Why do we know Hebrews 6:4-6 isn't saying a Christian can lose their salvation? (See page 119.)

14. First Peter 4:17 encourages us to examine ourselves, and Hebrews 4:12 says God's Word is able to discern our actions and motives.

a. Why is self-examination important even when we're genuinely saved?

b. What are some of the benefits of frequent self-examination?

They Go from Bad to Worse

15. What was Balaam's motive for helping a pagan king? (See page 122.)

16. Because Balaam couldn't curse Israel, what did he tell Balak to do? (See page 123.)

17. Read 1 Timothy 6:10. What is one reason some people stray from the faith?

18. Is money evil? Explain. (See pages 123-124.)

FORTIFY YOURSELF

19. Below, write a brief list of five ways you can fortify yourself. (See page 125.)

 a.

b.

c.

d.

e.

PUTTING YOUR BOLD STAND INTO ACTION

20. Why do you think the Bible goes into such great detail to describe what false teachers are like?

21. One of the ways we can fortify ourselves against false teaching is to take Philippians 4:8 to heart: "Whatever things are true, whatever things are noble, whatever things are just, whatever things are pure, whatever things are lovely, whatever things are of good report, if there is any virtue and if there is anything praiseworthy—meditate on these things." Why do you think it's so vital for us to guard our thought life?

22. In 1 Timothy 6:11-12, Paul wrote, "You, O man of God...pursue righteousness, godliness, faith, love, patience, gentleness. Fight the good fight of faith." Think about a time in the past when you fought the good fight of faith. How did God use that experience to help you grow more spiritually mature?

LESSON 8

IT'S DARK OUT THERE

> Today, you and I are navigating rocky, bumpy and spiritually slippery roads where we'll encounter false doctrine, false teachers, demonic activity, and satanic worship. If we're going to survive these dangerous conditions, we need to have a greater understanding of what we're dealing with.
>
> *Called to Take a Bold Stand*, page 128

Have you ever noticed how often God calls us to be diligent about guarding the truth and avoiding error? Paul exhorted Timothy to "guard what was committed to your trust, avoiding the profane and idle babblings and contradictions of what is falsely called knowledge" (1 Timothy 6:20).

Speaking about the truth, Paul also said, "Hold fast to the pattern of sound words which you have heard from me, in faith and love which are in Christ Jesus. That good thing which was committed to you, keep by the Holy Spirit who dwells in us" (2 Timothy 1:14).

We've already seen how Jude 1:3 commands us to "contend earnestly for the faith." First Peter 3:15 says we are to "always be ready to give a defense to everyone who asks [us] a reason for the hope that is in [us], with meekness and fear."

God wants us to be ready and proactive. We're to make sure our lives line up with biblical doctrine. First Timothy 4:16 says, "Take heed to yourself and to the doctrine. Continue in them, for in doing this you will save both yourself and those who hear you."

The common thread that runs through these verses and many more is that Christ wants a church that preserves and protects the truth. We should earnestly take to heart the command in 2 Timothy 2:15: "Be diligent to present yourself approved to God, a worker who does not need to be ashamed, rightly dividing the word of truth."

The more that we are careful to rightly divide God's Word, the better we will be able to navigate the hazards that false teachers are bringing into the church.

GROWING BOLDER

As you answer the following questions, you'll want to have your Bible in hand, as well as your copy of the book *Called to Take a Bold Stand.*

THE DARK REALM

1. Who are our true enemies? (See page 129.)

2. On page 130 of *Called to Take a Bold Stand*, we read, "Satan wants nothing more than to see churches full of uninformed believers." Why is this the case?

3. What incident in Daniel 10:12-13 informs us of how demonic forces operate in the unseen world?

THE FALLEN ANGELS

4. What happened to Lucifer that led to him becoming Satan? (See page 133.)

5. What does Revelation 12:4, 9 tell us about the extent of Satan's revolt? (See page 133.)

6. In general, fallen angels are able to disrupt our lives. But according to 2 Peter 2:4, what condemnation did God place upon a specific group of fallen angels?

7. According to Jude 1:6-7, what had these angels done to deserve such punishment? (See pages 134-135.)

8. While it is possible for fallen angels to cause trouble for us, it is not possible for them to possess us. In what ways do the following verses affirm this?

   a. 2 Corinthians 6:15—

   b. Ephesians 4:30—

   c. Colossians 1:13-14—

   d. 1 John 4:4—

9. What instructions does the Bible give to us about the devil?

a. James 4:7—

b. 1 Peter 5:8-9—

10. What did Genesis 3:15 say Satan would do to Jesus at the cross? And what would Jesus do to Satan? (See pages 137-138.)

11. With Christ's victory at the cross, what happened, according to Colossians 2:15?

THE DAYS OF NOAH: THEN AND NOW

12. For what reasons did God destroy the whole earth by flood? (See page 139.)

13. What warning did Jesus give about the future in Matthew 24:37? (See page 139.)

14. In what ways do you see today's world as being similar to the world Noah lived in?

LIGHT WILL WIN

15. Below, write two or three examples of the ways that the realms of righteousness and wickedness are clashing with each other today.

16. What does 1 Corinthians 10:4 say about the weapons of our warfare?

17. What are we to do with every thought, according to verse 5?

18. Christians have no reason to be fearful of God's judgment upon unbelievers. What guarantee do we have of this, according to Ephesians 1:13-14?

PUTTING YOUR BOLD STAND INTO ACTION

19. In what ways are we to be alert against false teachers, Satan and his influence, and sin?

    a. 1 Thessalonians 5:21-22—

    b. 1 Peter 5:8—

c. 1 John 2:15-17—

d. 1 John 4:1—

20. What resources has God given us to help protect us in the battle against false teachings and sin?

a. Psalm 119:11—

b. John 14:26—

c. Ephesians 6:10-18—

21. Read Romans 8:35, 38-39, then answer the questions that follow:

Who shall separate us from the love of Christ? Shall tribulation, or distress, or persecution, or famine, or nakedness, or peril, or sword?...For I am persuaded that neither death nor life, nor angels nor principalities nor powers, nor things present nor things to come, nor height nor depth, nor any other created thing, shall be able to separate us from the love of God which is in Christ Jesus our Lord.

a. What does this passage communicate about the security of your salvation?

b. To what extent do you think God is committed to upholding and protecting you?

c. In what ways does this passage comfort or encourage you?

LESSON 9

URGENT, URGENT, URGENT!

> In the last chapter, we saw how the sway of the dark realm potentially influences believers and unbelievers alike. The awareness of the dark realm's reach should galvanize us with a sense of urgency to actively share God's concern about where people will spend eternity.
>
> *Called to Take a Bold Stand*, page 145

As long as unbelievers are alive, they have time to make a choice about where they will spend eternity. But the moment a person dies, time has run out. There is no second chance for him or her to change their mind. As Hebrews 9:27 says, "It is appointed for men to die once, but after this the judgment."

For every unbeliever, the clock is ticking. And no one knows, in advance, how much time they have left before they die. Death is unpredictable, which means that we who are Christians should always have a sense of urgency when it comes to warning unbelievers of the eternal consequences of their sin.

As long as we remain here on this planet, God's main purpose for us is to shine His light into the darkness by proclaiming the gospel and drawing people to Christ through our words and actions. As 2 Corinthians 5:20 says, "We are ambassadors for Christ," and we are to exhort unbelievers to be "reconciled to God."

An ambassador is someone who represents his or her own country in a foreign land. As

Christians, we are pilgrims in a foreign realm. And as citizens of heaven (Philippians 3:20), we are ambassadors for Christ here on Earth.

To be appointed a political ambassador is considered an honor. To be appointed a spiritual ambassador is an even greater honor!

GROWING BOLDER

As you answer the following questions, you'll want to have your Bible in hand, as well as your copy of the book *Called to Take a Bold Stand.*

AN URGENT CALL

1. What is God's attitude toward the lost, according to 2 Peter 3:9?

2. What do the following passages say about the price God was willing to pay to make salvation possible for unbelievers?

   a. John 3:16—

   b. Romans 5:8—

   c. 2 Corinthians 5:21—

   d. 1 Peter 2:24—

3. In a vision, Isaiah was brought before God's throne. What question did God ask in Isaiah 6:8? How did Isaiah respond?

4. On page 147 of *Called to Take a Bold Stand*, we read, "Once you fully grasp the depth of God's forgiveness, you are willing to do whatever God asks." Why do you think this is the case?

5. As Christians, we are on mission. Read 2 Timothy 2:3-4.

   a. What exhortation are we given in verse 3?

   b. What does verse 4 say about our calling?

6. What are some reasons that we lose our sense of urgency about sharing the gospel and making disciples?

AN URGENT MESSAGE

7. When it comes to the choices we make in life, what are some things we do that end up hurting our testimony to unbelievers?

8. What kinds of choices help us to stand out as radically different than unbelievers?

9. What does it mean to "stop looking over your shoulder spiritually"? (See page 151.)

10. On page 151 of *Called to Take a Bold Stand*, we read that "Noah's whole life was like a town crier or heralder shouting a clear message to those around him." How can we as Christians be more deliberate about what our life says to others even during our shortest encounters with them, such as a bank clerk, a cashier, a parking lot attendant, a waiter or waitress, or other such individuals?

11. As Christians, we face the risk that unbelievers will lie about us or accuse us of wrong. What do the following passages say about our response to false accusations?

    a. Matthew 5:11-12—

    b. 1 Peter 3:9—

    c. 1 Peter 3:16—

    d. 1 Peter 4:15-16—

12. What does it mean for us to preach both "mercy and judgment"? (See page 153.)

AN URGENT WARNING FOR TODAY

13. How has God used Sodom and Gomorrah, according to 2 Peter 2:6?

14. Read Ephesians 5:8. What was true about us at one time, and what exhortation are we given now that we're believers?

BE GOD'S MESSENGER OF MERCY AND GRACE

15. We're called to carry heaven's influence to all the places we traffic. What are two or three new ways you can be more intentional about this in your life?

PUTTING YOUR BOLD STAND INTO ACTION

16. On page 152 of *Called to Take a Bold Stand*, we read, "Sometimes people won't listen. It takes wisdom to know when to use words and when to let our actions do the talking."

    a. Give two or three examples of times when actions may be better than words.

b. What kinds of actions do you think would attract the attention of unbelievers?

17. Ephesians 4:15 urges us, in our encounters with others, to speak the truth in love.

    a. What danger is there in speaking the truth without love?

    b. What danger is there in speaking with love, but omitting truth?

    c. Why are both love and truth so essential?

18. Have you had any recent experiences in which, after you interacted with an unbeliever, you wish you had handled the situation differently? What did you learn from that incident, and how can you prepare to do better next time?

LESSON 10

THE FALSE AND THE TRUE

> We would do well to remember three areas vulnerable to demonic attack. The first is religion. Satan loves to infiltrate religious settings in his quest to deceive. But if someone isn't interested in religion, that's okay. He has another line of attack—politics. Globally, nations are cracking under the strain of recent events, and in response, leaders are ushering in ideologies promising a collective utopia that human nature renders impossible. Yet citizens looking to replace God with government as the provider of every need are falling for this deception wholesale. And then there are the dark powers present in the realm of business. Satan makes it a point to move among the movers and shakers of the business world.
>
> *Called to Take a Bold Stand,* page 162

Satan's influence is pervasive. He is a determined foe. That's why 1 Peter 5:8 warns us to "be sober, be vigilant, because your adversary the devil walks about like a roaring lion, seeking whom he may devour." Ephesians 2:2 describes Satan as "the prince of the power of the air, the spirit who now works in the sons of disobedience." As the ruler of this world, he is eager to spread evil and darkness in every way possible.

When Satan does his work, he's not blatant. He packages himself attractively and "transforms himself into an angel of light" (2 Corinthians 11:14). When he tempts people, he makes the temptation look inviting and promises fulfillment. He appeals to people's desires and shrouds his poisonous lies so that his prospective victims are unable to recognize they are being deceived.

One of Satan's most frequent strategies is to get people to doubt God. That's how he caused Adam and Eve to fall into sin in the garden of Eden—a sin that led to the fall of all mankind. Other tactics include filling people's hearts with fear or guilt. He has plenty of tools to use in his efforts to make us stumble, which is why it's so vital for us to live in a constant state of awareness.

GROWING BOLDER

As you answer the following questions, you'll want to have your Bible in hand, as well as your copy of the book *Called to Take a Bold Stand.*

EMPTY AND DRY

1. Against what does Satan aim his most virulent attacks? (See page 163.)

2. Why is it so difficult for us to recognize false apostles, deceitful workers, and even Satan, according to 2 Corinthians 11:13-15?

3. How does 2 Peter 2:17 describe false leaders? What does this tell us about them? (See page 163.)

4. What additional information does Jude 1:12 give us about false teachers?

LEGALISTIC HYPOCRITES

5. How does spiritual dryness often manifest itself? (See page 164.)

6. What did Jesus warn against in Luke 12:1? (See page 165.)

7. What is the right way to view the Ten Commandments? (See page 165.)

8. What is the wrong way to view the Ten Commandments? (See page 165.)

9. What is legalism? (See page 165 and Galatians 2:16.)

10. How does salvation come? (See page 167.)

11. In contrast, what do cults and false teachers want us to do, and why? (See page 167.)

12. What is the antidote to legalism? (See page 167 and 2 Timothy 3:16.)

MASTERS OF ENSLAVEMENT

13. What is one of the great crimes Satan perpetuates against humanity? (See page 168.)

14. When false teachers promise liberty, what are they actually offering? (See page 168.)

15. What is true biblical liberty? Explain. (See pages 168-169.)

16. Why is following a false teacher like stepping into wet concrete? (See page 169.)

JUSTICE IS COMING!

17. What future has God planned for false teachers, according to 2 Peter 2:17?

18. What does Proverbs 19:5 promise to those who promote falsehood?

STAND, PERSEVERE, AND ADVANCE

19. What is our Christian freedom synonymous with? (See page 172.)

20. What is real Christian liberty, and what is it not? (See page 173.)

21. Does the fact we are experiencing hardship mean we are not useful to God? (See pages 175-176.)

22. What mindset should we have, according to Philippians 3:12-14?

PUTTING YOUR BOLD STAND INTO ACTION

23. On page 169 of *Called to Take a Bold Stand*, we read that "Satan is a gradualist." What does this mean? What can we do to make sure we're not gradually seduced by false teachers or Satan?

24. Philippians 3:12-14 is rich with practical application, so let's revisit it here:

> Not that I have already attained, or am already perfected; but I press on, that I may lay hold of that for which Christ Jesus has also laid hold of me. Brethren, I do not count myself to have apprehended; but one thing I do, forgetting those things which are behind and reaching forward to those things which are ahead, I press toward the goal for the prize of the upward call of God in Christ Jesus.

a. What attitude or perspective is conveyed by Paul's statement "I press on"?

b. What did Paul forget, and what did he reach forward to?

c. What goal did Paul pursue?

d. Based on what Paul wrote, how would you characterize the manner in which he approached the Christian life?

25. At the end of his life, Paul was able to write, "I have finished the race, I have kept the faith" (2 Timothy 4:7). What do you think are the keys to making sure you finish well?

PART 3

GOING PUBLIC

LESSON 11

WHAT ARE YOU WAITING FOR?

The Bible says that people are spiritually quickened or made alive when they are born again and will be physically quickened at the resurrection. Now, ask yourself: "Are there signs that events are accelerating before us, moving us toward the end of the age? Is there a tension that seems to indicate God is about to intervene in our lives?" I would say yes! This quickening is a reminder to the church of what is soon to come. And it is a tremendous time to be alive.

Called to Take a Bold Stand, page 179

Are you living with the expectation that your circumstances could change at any moment? World events are moving at a faster pace than ever before. New developments happen almost constantly, taking us by surprise. Life can take unexpected turns. We have no idea where we will be a month from now or a year from now. And most importantly of all, we don't know when the rapture will occur. It could happen at any time.

This is one of the reasons Ephesians 5:15-17 says, "See then that you walk circumspectly, not as fools but as wise, redeeming the time, because the days are evil. Therefore do not be unwise, but understand what the will of the Lord is."

We're called to understand—and do—the Lord's will. We're to be intentional about how we use our time because the days are evil and short. To be wise is to use our time well and to be purposeful about how we live.

The main reason God has not revealed the day and hour of the rapture is so that we're constantly motivated to be wise stewards of the time He has given to us. With that in mind, let's look at what the Bible says about the rapture.

GROWING BOLDER

As you answer the following questions, you'll want to have your Bible in hand, as well as your copy of the book *Called to Take a Bold Stand.*

1. Have people been raptured before? Explain. (See page 180.)

2. What happens when people in the church arm themselves with the hope of the rapture? (See page 180.)

3. What perspective do the following passages say we should have about the rapture?

   a. 1 Thessalonians 5:6—

   b. Hebrews 9:28—

IS THE RAPTURE BIBLICAL?

4. How do we respond to those who say the word *rapture* doesn't appear in our English Bibles? (See page 181.)

5. Who introduced the doctrine of the rapture in John 14:1-3? (See page 181.)

6. In 1 Corinthians 15:51, what does the word "mystery" mean? (See page 182.)

7. In the same passage, what does "sleep" refer to? (See page 182.)

8. Now read 1 Corinthians 15:51-53. What will happen at the rapture, and how quickly will it take place?

9. Read 1 Thessalonians 1:10 and 5:9. What is one of the purposes of the rapture?

WHAT ABOUT BELIEVERS WHO DIE BEFORE THE RAPTURE?

10. What happens to a believer's spirit when the body dies, according to 2 Corinthians 5:8?

11. What will happen to the bodies of dead believers when the rapture takes place? (See page 184.)

12. What will happen to those who are still alive on Earth at the time of the rapture? (See page 184.)

THE RAPTURE ASSURES DELIVERANCE

13. Which nation is the star of the entire Bible? (See page 185.)

14. Even though Israel rejected God all through biblical history, what will eventually happen to Israel, according to the following passages?

    a. Zechariah 12:10—

    b. Romans 11:26—

15. What promises are given to Christians in the two passages listed below?

    a. John 5:24—

    b. 2 Peter 2:9—

16. What evidence do we see in Revelation 4:1-3 that supports the fact Christians will not experience God's wrath during the tribulation? (See page 187.)

17. Where is the church during the span from Revelation 4:1 to Revelation 19:11? (See page 188.)

18. Where will the church be at the time of Christ's second coming, according to Revelation 19:11-16?

19. Review the differences between the rapture and the second coming, as featured in the chart on pages 189-190. What four major differences do we see?

    a.

    b.

    c.

    d.

THE RAPTURE MOTIVATES

20. What "greatest motivator ever" do we have for what we do? (See page 190.)

21. In Romans 13:11-12, what are we exhorted to do?

22. According to Luke 12:37, who will be blessed?

23. As we wait for the rapture, what are we to do, according to Luke 19:13? (See page 192.)

PUTTING YOUR BOLD STAND INTO ACTION

24. First John 3:2-3 says, "Beloved, now we are children of God; and it has not yet been revealed what we shall be, but we know that when He is revealed, we shall be like Him, for we shall see Him as He is. And everyone who has this hope in Him purifies himself, just as He is pure."

    a. What does the person who lives in anticipation of the rapture do?

    b. Two key aspects of being ready for the rapture are having a clear conscience and not allowing sin to take hold in our lives. With that in mind, what do the following passages encourage us to do?

        Psalm 139:23-24—

        2 Corinthians 13:5—

        1 Peter 1:13—

1 John 1:9—

25. Hebrews 10:24-25 (NLT) tells us how we are to live as we see Christ's return drawing nearer: "Let us think of ways to motivate one another to acts of love and good works. And let us not neglect our meeting together, as some people do, but encourage one another, especially now that the day of His return is drawing near."

    a. Why do you think this kind of interaction with fellow believers is so vital?

    b. What is one way you can take steps to put the exhortation in Hebrews 10:24-25 into practice?

LESSON 12

TODAY IS THE BEST DAY

The condition of the world you and I live in makes it clear that no one, not our leaders nor the general public, knows what comes next. Only the God of the Bible knows the future, and before it comes to pass, He declared it (Isaiah 42:9). We know from Scripture that difficulties do lay ahead, yet God's prophetic Word serves as an encouragement for us to trust and believe that whatever happens does so under His watchful eye and sovereign control.

Called to Take a Bold Stand, page 197

God gave all of Scripture to us for a reason. From Genesis to Revelation, there are many truths He wants us to know, including truths about the future. Some churches don't teach the prophetic parts of the Bible because they feel that to do so invites sensationalism or controversy. But to ignore what God has revealed to us is to ignore information He deliberately included for our benefit.

There are many prophetic passages in the Bible that are relevant to what is happening in our world today. Again, God gave us this information for a reason. We have a responsibility to be good stewards of what God has entrusted to us, and that includes what He has chosen to let us know about the days in which we live.

We live in amazing times. The events we are witnessing today line up with what the prophets foretold in Scripture. This serves as powerful confirmation that we can trust the Bible. God alone knows the future, and it is unfolding exactly as He said it would. Let's learn more about what we should watch for!

GROWING BOLDER

As you answer the following questions, you'll want to have your Bible in hand, as well as your copy of the book *Called to Take a Bold Stand.*

IT'S A GOOD DAY TO BE ALIVE

1. How much of the Bible deals with eschatology, or the study of prophecy? (See page 196.) What does this say about the significance of this subject?

2. What is the difference between the end of the world and the end of the church on earth? (See page 197.)

IT'S A GOOD DAY TO KNOW YOU ARE LOVED

3. What does the word "beloved" in 2 Peter 3:1 convey about how God views us? (See page 198.)

4. What does 1 John 3:1 communicate about how God feels about us? (See page 198.)

IT'S A GOOD DAY TO BE REMINDED

5. In 2 Peter 3:1, Peter wrote that he wanted to "stir up [our] pure minds by way of reminder."

    a. What does the phrase "stir up" communicate? (See page 199.)

    b. When it comes to knowing God's Word, why do you think repetition is such a strong teacher? (See pages 199-200.)

6. What point did Paul make about repetition in Philippians 3:1? (See page 201.)

7. Read Psalm 139:17-18.

    a. Based on this passage, how often does God think about us?

    b. What does this tell you about God's love for you?

IT'S A GOOD DAY TO KNOW THE WITNESS OF GOD

8. What are witnesses called upon to do? (See page 202.)

9. According to 2 Peter 3:2, who were the apostles witnesses of? (See page 202.)

10. What did Stephen cover in his sermon recorded in Acts 7, and what point did he want to make to his captors? (See pages 203-204.)

11. What explains Stephen's courage to stand in the face of such opposition? (See page 204.)

IT'S A GOOD DAY TO GET READY

12. According to 2 Peter 3:4, what did Peter warn that scoffers would question in the last days? (See page 205.)

13. How do you think we can best prepare ourselves to answer such scoffers?

14. How does 2 Peter 3:16 define scoffers? (See page 205.)

15. When the Pharisees and Sadducees asked Jesus for a sign from heaven, He told them they were hypocrites. Why? (See pages 206-207.)

16. What point was Jesus making to the Pharisees and Sadducees when He mentioned the prophet Jonah? (See pages 206-207.)

IT'S A GOOD DAY TO GET WISE

17. Even though God gives ample evidence of His existence in nature, what do scoffers do, according to the beginning of 2 Peter 3:5? (See page 208.)

PUTTING YOUR BOLD STAND INTO ACTION

18. When you look at nature, what stands out to you as evidence for God's existence? List three or four examples below. Which one is your favorite, and why?

19. Second Peter 3:3-4 warns us that "scoffers will come in the last days...saying, 'Where is the promise of His coming?'" They will deny that Christ will return.

    In response, what Scripture passages can you cite that declare the certainty of Christ's coming? As you list the passages below, keep this important fact in mind: For every prophecy about Christ's first coming, there are eight about His second coming!

LESSON 13

HEADING FOR HOME

What do you think of when you hear the announcement, "I'm heading for home"? If you're a coach watching your runner round third base, there is a bit of nervous excitement. But if your boss says those same words at the end of a hectic 12-hour day, there's probably a sigh of relief. And how about the last day of vacation? Everybody knows it was a vacation away when they've had enough and want to go home. Thankfully, no matter how often we go home in this world, believers are not truly home yet. According to the Bible, God's people are pilgrims in a foreign land, and our hearts beat with longing for our real home, heaven.

Called to Take a Bold Stand, page 211

Because we've spent our entire lives in a fallen world filled with hurt, difficulties, pain, sin, and evil, it's hard for us to imagine just how wonderful heaven will be. We've never experienced what it's like to be in an environment that's free of the effects of sin. Heaven will be far more glorious than we expect.

Though we are used to living on this corrupt planet, because we are new creatures in Christ, we no longer feel at home here. We yearn for what is good and right. We long for the day when we will no longer struggle with temptation. We are eager to live under Christ's perfect rule rather than the jurisdiction of imperfect human governments. We grieve when we see people delight in wickedness and reject Christ and His truth. As those who love the things of God rather than the things of the world, we feel terribly out of place.

So it's natural that we want to learn as much as we can about heaven, our future home. Let's discover what Scripture tells us about heaven, where we will dwell with Christ forever.

GROWING BOLDER

As you answer the following questions, you'll want to have your Bible in hand, as well as your copy of the book *Called to Take a Bold Stand.*

HEAVEN IS WAITING

1. The Bible doesn't describe heaven as a sterile place with chubby angels plucking harps. What can we know about heaven with certainty, according to Revelation 22:3-5?

2. In heaven, we'll have the thrilling joy of meeting those whom we've read about in the Bible, including Moses, Ruth, David, Mary, and more. Who do you look forward to meeting, and why?

3. What assurance does Psalm 23:4 give to us? (See page 214.)

HEAVEN'S HOPE

4. On page 215 of *Called to Take a Bold Stand*, we read the question, "Is your heartbeat in sync with the heartbeat of the God of heaven?" What do you think are the advantages of being in sync with God's heartbeat?

5. In Romans 8:24, what is communicated by the fact the words "were saved" are in the past tense? (See page 215.)

6. In what ways do the following passages make it clear that our salvation is secure and our place in heaven is guaranteed?

   a. John 3:16—

   b. John 5:24—

   c. John 10:28-29—

   d. Ephesians 1:13-14—

   e. 1 John 2:25—

HEAVEN'S HELP

7. We don't have to wait until we get to heaven to receive God's help. What do the following passages tell us? (See page 216.)

   a. Psalm 121:2—

   b. Matthew 6:25-33—

8. In Romans 8:26, we read that "the Spirit also helps in our weaknesses." What is conveyed by the phrase "the Spirit...helps"? (See page 217.)

9. What does Jesus' quick response to Peter's short prayer communicate to us? (See page 218.)

HEAVEN'S CONFIDENCE

10. Read Romans 8:28-30. In what ways does this passage make you feel secure?

11. Even though our salvation is secure, what does Philippians 2:12 urge us to do? (See page 219.)

12. What happens when we make the mistake of "parking our faith"? (See page 220.)

13. What happens when we put faith to the test? (See page 220.)

HEAVEN'S OUTWORKING

14. What should we do when we find ourselves lacking motivation to do what Christ asks? (See page 221.)

15. What responsibility do we have when it comes to the gospel? (See page 222.)

16. What does 2 Corinthians 6:1-2 communicate about the gospel?

HEAVEN'S DEVOTION

17. On page 224 of *Called to Take a Bold Stand*, we read, "Practice living kingdom life here and now so that when God's kingdom comes, it isn't going to be much different for you." Where do you see room for growth as you practice living kingdom life? What command are we given in 2 Peter 3:18?

PUTTING YOUR BOLD STAND INTO ACTION

18. On pages 223-224 of *Called to Take a Bold Stand*, we read, "If you and I truly have faith, we will be serious about our faith right now and absolutely devoted to acting in accordance with God's very nature, purpose, and will." Keeping in mind that Christ could return at any time, how do the following passages exhort us to live?

    a. Matthew 9:37-38—

    b. Romans 12:11—

    c. Ephesians 5:15-17—

    d. Colossians 4:5-6—

19. Are you able to communicate the gospel clearly and simply to an unbeliever? What does an unbeliever need to know to have a clear understanding of his or her status before God, and the need for salvation in Christ? Write out the essential points of the gospel message here:

    a. Romans 3:23—

    b. Romans 6:23—

c. Romans 5:8—

d. Romans 10:9-10—

e. Ephesians 2:8-9—

20. Sometime today, take time to pray and ask the Lord, "How can I fulfill Your command to occupy until You come?" As you do this, consider how God is using you right now in your sphere of influence. How could you make yourself more available to Him?

LESSON 14

BEFORE I LET YOU GO

> Before I let you go, it is essential to look at the Holy Spirit's association with the Christian's bold faith because such faith is impossible without Him. We cannot and will not survive without a fresh infusion of the power, the purpose, and the Person of God, the Holy Spirit. Believer, the same exceedingly great power that raised Christ from the dead is at work in you! (Ephesians 1:19-20).
>
> *Called to Take a Bold Stand*, page 227

Every believer possesses the Holy Spirit. He dwells in us and empowers us to fulfill the callings of the Christian life. It is the Spirit who convicts people of sin (John 16:7-9) and transforms believers to become like Christ (2 Corinthians 3:18). The Spirit is the one who guides us in all truth (John 14:26) and equips us to minister to fellow believers (1 Corinthians 12:4-11; Ephesians 4:11-16). As the Spirit works through us, He builds up the church (Ephesians 2:22), and He enables us to bear the fruit of the Spirit (Galatians 5:22-23).

This tells us how vital it is for us to walk in the Spirit and allow Him to do His empowering work through us! Only with His help are we able to live spiritually productive lives.

GROWING BOLDER

As you answer the following questions, you'll want to have your Bible in hand, as well as your copy of the book *Called to Take a Bold Stand.*

THE HOLY SPIRIT IN HISTORY

1. Very briefly, how have we seen the Holy Spirit at work in Bible times and church history? (See pages 228-230.)

THE HOLY SPIRIT IS KNOWABLE

2. What do the following passages tell us about the Holy Spirit? (See pages 230-231.)

   a. 1 Corinthians 2:10-11—

   b. Ephesians 4:30—

   c. 1 Corinthians 12:11—

   d. John 15:26—

   e. 2 Peter 1:21—

f. John 14:26—

g. Romans 8:26—

3. What traits does the Holy Spirit possess that reveal He is divine? (See page 231.)

   a. 1 Corinthians 2:10-11—

   b. Psalm 139:7—

   c. Genesis 1:2—

   d. 1 John 5:6—

4. What does today's resistance to the Holy Spirit explain? (See page 232.)

THE HOLY SPIRIT'S EMPOWERMENT

5. What was the result when the Holy Spirit came upon the believers who were in the upper room? (See Acts 2:1-4 and page 233.)

6. In what ways have you sensed the Holy Spirit's empowerment or leading during your times of private worship or when you get together with fellow believers?

THE HOLY SPIRIT PUTS FAITH TO WORK

7. On page 234 of *Called to Take a Bold Stand*, we read, "Faith becomes practical, usable, and enduring when faith in Jesus Christ is brought together with God's Word and the power of the Holy Spirit in conjunction with the will of the Father." Why do you think it is so important for us to be (1) active in our faith, (2) consistently in the Word, and (3) constantly reliant upon the Spirit's power as we go about our daily lives?

THE HOLY SPIRIT COMMISSIONS

8. What is the word *commissioning* often used to speak of in Christian circles? (See page 237.)

9. What commission did Jesus receive as He prayed in the Garden of Gethsemane? (See page 237.)

10. What commissioning did Jesus give to His apostles—and to all believers through the ages—in Matthew 28:19-20?

COMMISSIONED FOR RIGHTEOUSNESS'S SAKE

11. When Jesus proclaimed His commission, what promise did He give to us, according to Matthew 28:20? (See page 241.)

12. Why are we able to exercise bold faith? (See page 241.)

PUTTING YOUR BOLD STAND INTO ACTION

13. Romans 12:1-2 (NIV) gives us this important exhortation: "I urge you, brothers and sisters, in view of God's mercy, to offer your bodies as a living sacrifice, holy and pleasing to God—this is your true and proper worship. Do not conform to the pattern of this world, but be transformed by the renewing of your mind. Then you will be able to test and approve what God's will is—His good, pleasing and perfect will."

    a. What do you think it means to offer yourself to God as a "living sacrifice"?

    b. What would you say are the essentials for renewing our minds? As you respond, consider what is said in John 17:17, Philippians 4:8, and 2 Timothy 3:16-17.

14. On page 240 of *Called to Take a Bold Stand*, we read, "The choices that you and I make set in motion the kind of life we will live. Will it be a transformed life of faith, or something less? By choosing to exercise biblical faith, your life will not be stationary nor static. It's impossible. Why? Because as children of the living God, we are in this world to spread His love, grace, and message."

    a. Why do you think there is such a strong connection between the choices we make and the kind of impact we have on other people's lives?

    b. In your own life, what two or three kinds of choices do you think have the greatest bearing on your spiritual growth and fruitfulness?

    c. Below, list some specific ways you would like to spread God's love, grace, and message to others. Then take time to pray over each item in your list, and tell God you want to make yourself fully available for His use and the Spirit's empowerment as you act upon what you've written below.

OTHER GREAT READING BY JACK HIBBS

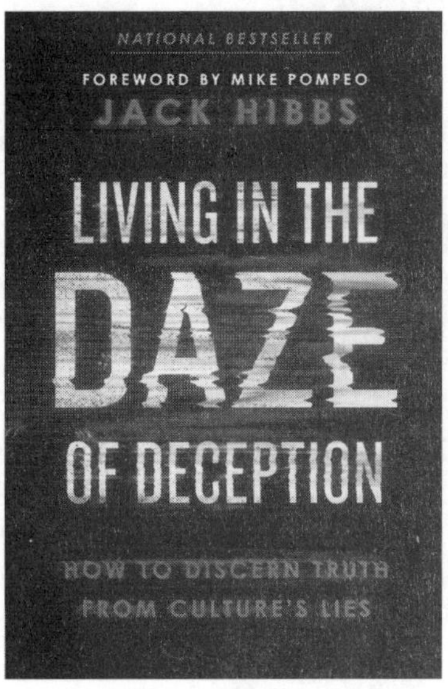

A HIGH-STAKES BATTLE FOR EVERY CHRISTIAN

Jesus warned that deception would grow worse as we draw nearer to the end times, saying, "Take heed that no one deceives you" (Matthew 24:4). Distinguishing truth from error has become an increasingly challenging task—even in the church.

We live in a time when falsehoods assault us from every direction. Packaged with just enough truth to make them appear trustworthy, these counterfeits have grown more and more difficult to detect and avoid.

Living in the Daze of Deception explores the many ways error is masquerading as truth—and how you can discern the difference. From pastor Jack Hibbs, you'll learn

- the characteristics of deceivers and how they have brought harm to both secular culture and the church
- the many deceptions that are altering and replacing the truth, and how to recognize them
- the keys to standing strong as the spiritual battles surrounding us intensify

The greatest antidote to deception is truth. Equip yourself now to grow in discernment so that you can protect yourself from error and remain steadfast in your faith!

ARMING YOURSELF WITH GOD'S TRUTH IN A WORLD FULL OF LIES

Not a day goes by without falsehoods of one kind or another besieging us. Because they are often packaged with just enough truth to make them appear trustworthy, we're called to be vigilant and discerning.

In this companion workbook to *Living in the Daze of Deception*, pastor Jack Hibbs enables you to distinguish error from that which is good and right. In this informative resource, you will

- learn how to recognize different kinds of deception and how they fall short of God's truth
- explore scenarios in which deception takes place and how to best respond with wisdom, prayer, and conviction
- equip yourself with the tools God has provided for your spiritual protection and be encouraged to thrive in the face of opposition

This powerful guide will embolden you more than ever to stand strong and shine God's light into a dark world! And you'll know the confidence and peace that comes from anchoring your life in God's truth.

To learn more about Harvest House books and to read sample chapters, visit our website:

www.HarvestHousePublishers.com